Viola Time Runners

a second book of easy pieces fo...

Kathy and David Blackwell

Illustrations by

Martin Remphry

Welcome to **Viola Time Runners**. You'll find:

- pieces using the finger patterns 0–12–3–4 and 0–1–2–34
- duets, with parts of equal difficulty
- two new pieces, replacing nos. 11 and 16
- a Music Fact-Finder Page at the back to help explain words and signs
- play-along tracks and lively and characterful accompaniments available to download from **www.oup.com/vtrunners2e** or to stream on major streaming platforms
- straightforward piano and viola accompaniments available separately
- a book for viola that's also compatible with Fiddle Time Runners

Teacher's note:

All the pieces in *Viola Time Runners* with the exception of the C string specials can be played together with *Fiddle Time Runners*. There are a few additional pieces in *Fiddle Time Runners* that are not included in the viola book.

 denotes a part that fits with Fiddle Time Runners: these are printed in sequence in the book or on page 30–5. The audio tracks for the pieces listed as 'ensemble parts' are played first by viola and piano, then with the violin part added.

C string special denotes pieces that provide practice on the C string.

OXFORD
UNIVERSITY PRESS

Great Clarendon Street, Oxford OX2 6DP, England
This collection © Oxford University Press 2005 and 2023.
Unless marked otherwise, all pieces are by Kathy and David Blackwell and are
© Oxford University Press. All traditional pieces, and nos. 9, 10, 12, 13, 14, 23, 24, and 30 are
arranged by Kathy and David Blackwell and are © Oxford University Press.
Unauthorized arrangement or photocopying of this copyright material is ILLEGAL.
Kathy and David Blackwell have asserted their right under the Copyright,
Designs and Patents Act, 1988, to be identified as the Composers of this Work.
Impression: 1
ISBN: 978-0-19-356619-4
Music and text origination by Julia Bovee
Printed in Great Britain

Contents

New notes for 2nd finger

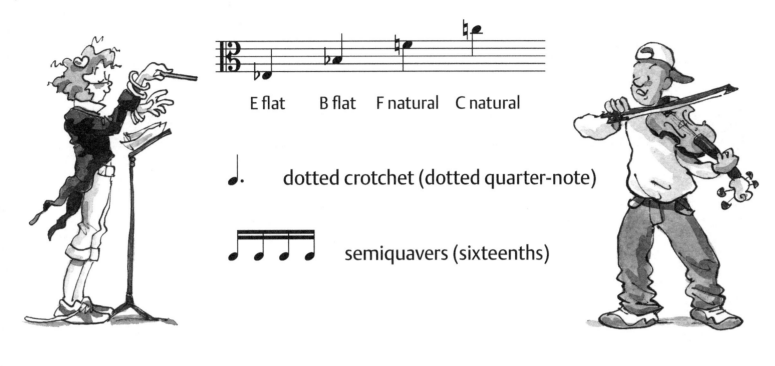

E flat   B flat   F natural   C natural

♩.   dotted crotchet (dotted quarter-note)

    semiquavers (sixteenths)

1. Start the show

Count 4 bars

Rock tempo

KB & DB

2. Banyan tree

C string special

Jamaican folk tune

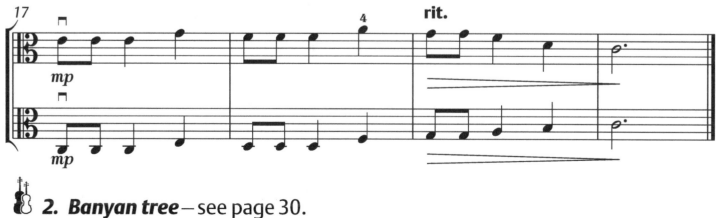

2. Banyan tree – see page 30.

3. Heat haze

KB & DB

To practise the main rhythm of this piece, try saying

'Hot   and sun - ny.'

4. Medieval tale

KB & DB

🎻 **4. Medieval tale** – see page 30.

5. **Cornish May song** — see page 30.

7. Merrily danced the Quaker's wife

Scottish folk tune

7. Merrily danced the Quaker's wife
(ensemble part)

Scottish folk tune

8. *O leave your sheep*

C string special

French folk tune

8. *O leave your sheep* — see page 31.

9. Jingle bells

10. Allegretto in C

Allegretto

Mozart

mf

 **10. Allegretto in G** — see page 31.

11. The Mallow fling

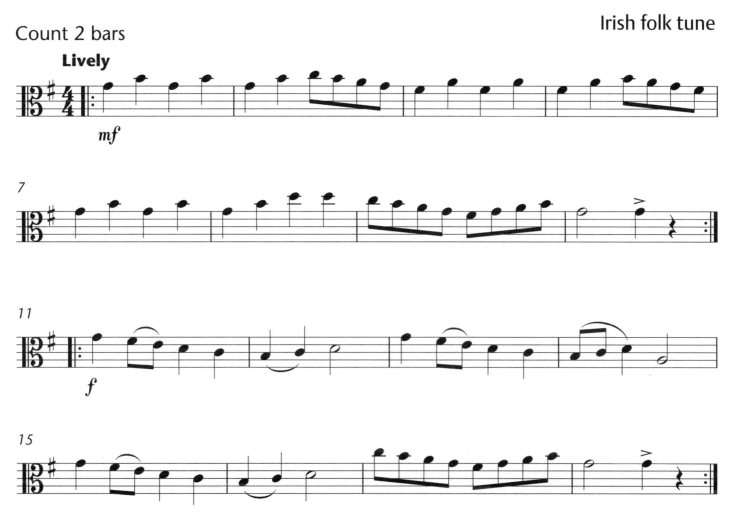

Irish folk tune

Count 2 bars

Lively

mf

f

12. Noël

C string special

Daquin

Allegretto

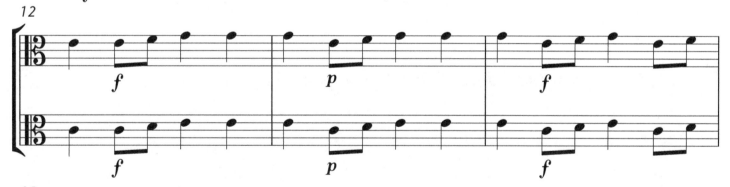

12. Noël — see page 32.

13. Finale from the 'Water Music'

Handel

13. **Finale from the 'Water Music'** – see page 32.

14. Ecossaise in G

(ensemble part)

Beethoven

15. Viola Time rag

Count 4 bars

KB & DB

16. Busy day

KB & DB

Busily

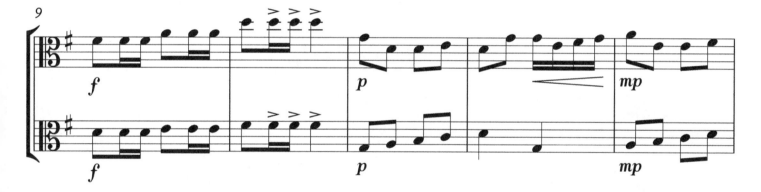

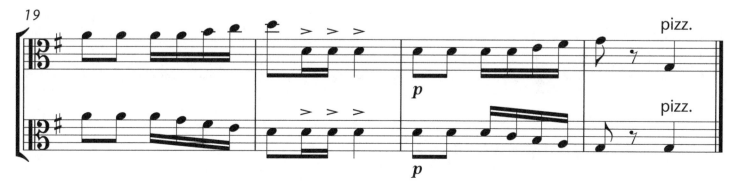

17. On the go!

Count 4 bars

KB & DB

18. Blue whale

C string special

KB & DB

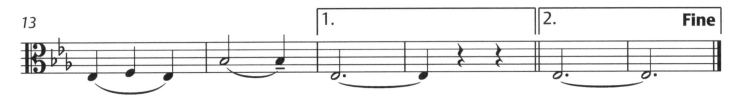

 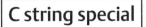

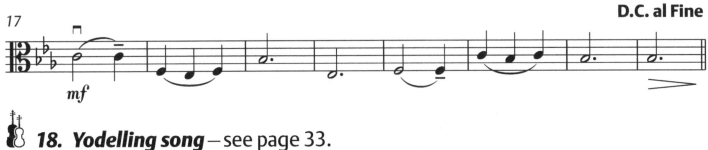

18. Yodelling song — see page 33.

19. Takin' it easy

Count 4 bars

Laid-back tempo

KB & DB

mp legato

20. Mean street chase

C string special

Funky

KB & DB

20. *Romani band*—see page 33.

21. Ten thousand miles away

C string special

Sea shanty

With a good swing

Fine

18

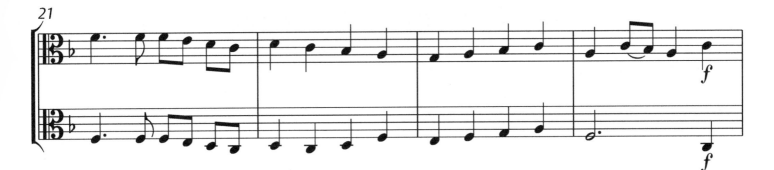

D.C. al Fine

 21. Ten thousand miles away
(lower part of violin duet)

With a good swing

Sea shanty

22. I got those viola blues

This is the octave harmonic on the A string.

23. Air in C

J. C. Bach

Andante

mf

mp

mf cresc.

f

 **23. Air in G** — see page 34.

24. Prelude from 'Te Deum'

Charpentier

Maestoso

f

mp

cresc.

f

rit.

ff

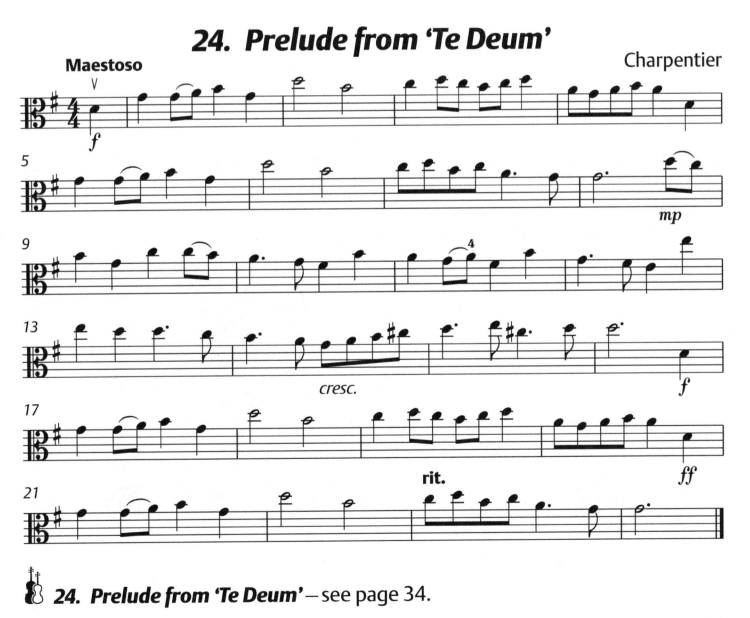 **24. Prelude from 'Te Deum'** — see page 34.

25. That's how it goes!

Luckily, this piece is not as hard as it looks!

New notes for 3rd finger

F sharp   C sharp   G sharp

26. Flamenco dance
(*FTR* No. 28)

KB & DB

27. Somebody's knocking at your door

(**FTR** No. 30)

Spiritual

28. The old chariot

Sea shanty

31. The old chariot
(ensemble part)

Sea shanty

29. Adam in the garden

30. Air

Handel

32. Air — see page 35.

31. The wee cooper o' Fife

(*FTR* No. 33; adapted melody)

Scottish folk tune

32. Aerobics!

KB & DB

🎻 *37. Aerobics!* — see page 35.

33. Caribbean sunshine

(*FTR* No. 38; ensemble part)

KB & DB

These additional parts are compatible with, and are numbered as, the pieces in *Fiddle Time Runners*.

2. Banyan tree
(lower part of violin duet)

Jamaican folk tune

4. Medieval tale
(ensemble part)

KB & DB

5. Cornish May song
(ensemble part)

Cornish folk tune

8. O leave your sheep
(lower part of violin duet)

French folk tune

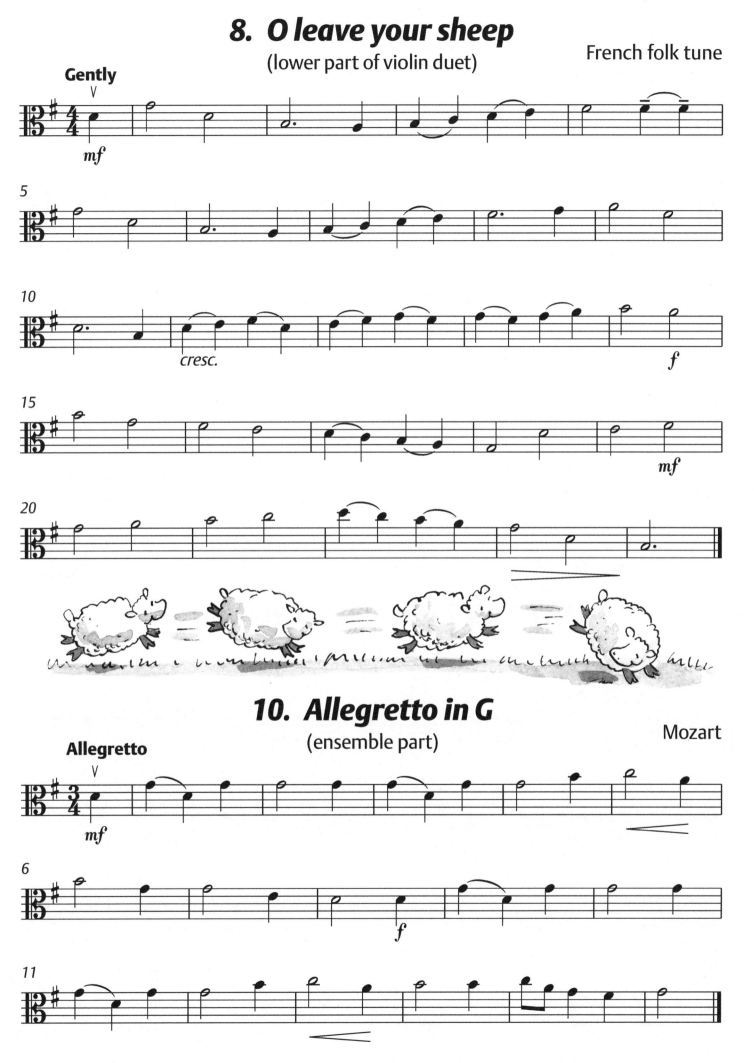

10. Allegretto in G
(ensemble part)

Mozart

12. Noël
(lower part of violin duet)

Daquin

13. Finale from the 'Water Music'
(ensemble part)

Handel

(rall. 2nd time)

18. Yodelling song
(melody)

German folk tune

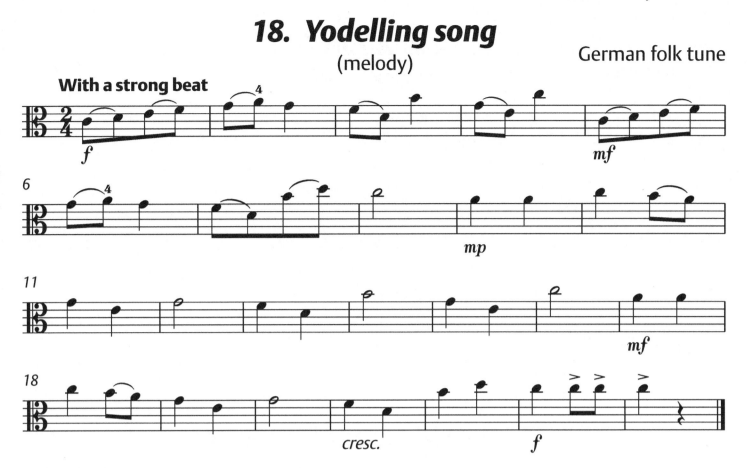

20. Romani band
(melody)

KB & DB

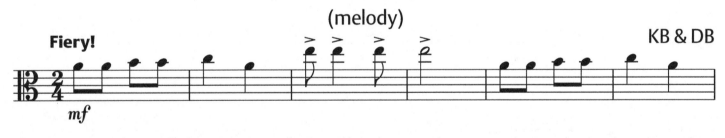

23. Air in G

(ensemble part)

J. C. Bach

24. Prelude from 'Te Deum'

(ensemble part)

Charpentier

32. Air
(ensemble part for violin duet)

Handel

* Play these notes if the second violin part isn't played.

37. Aerobics!
(ensemble part)

KB & DB

Music Fact-Finder Page

Here are some of the words and signs you will find in some of your pieces!

How to play it

pizzicato or pizz. = pluck

arco = with the bow

⊓ = down bow

V = up bow

> = accent

𝄃 = tremolo

Don't get lost!

‖: :‖ = repeat marks

|1. |2. | = first and second time bars

D.C. al Fine = repeat from the beginning and stop at **Fine**

D.% al Fine = repeat from the sign % and stop at **Fine**

rit. or **rall.** = gradually getting slower

a tempo = back to the first speed

⌒ = pause

Volume control

p (*piano*) = quiet

mp (*mezzo-piano*) = moderately quiet

mf (*mezzo-forte*) = moderately loud

f (*forte*) = loud

ff (*fortissimo*) = very loud

_____ or *crescendo* (*cresc.*) = getting gradually louder

_____ or *diminuendo* (*dim.*) = getting gradually quieter

Italian phrase-book

Allegro = fast and lively

Allegretto = not too fast

Andante = at a walking pace

legato = smoothly

Maestoso = majestically

Moderato = at a moderate speed

Practissimo = lots of Viola Time!